221.9   (K-4)   3-4
B
c. 1   BULLA, CLYDE R

JONAH AND THE
GREAT FISH

2004

JONAH AND THE
GREAT FISH

JONAH AND THE GREAT FISH

By CLYDE ROBERT BULLA

Illustrated by Helga Aichinger

THOMAS Y. CROWELL COMPANY *New York*

Illustrations copyright © 1970 by Helga Aichinger

Printed in the Netherlands.

L.C. Card 69-13636

For Esther, Walter,
Debbie, and David

Jonah and the Great Fish

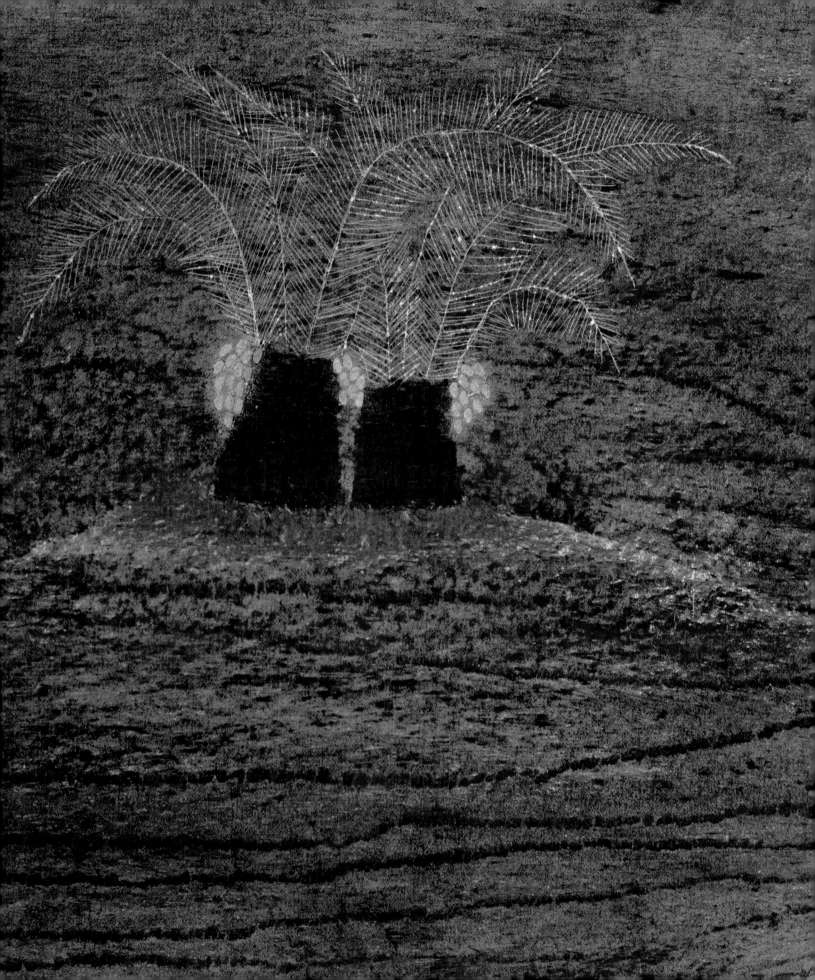

LONG AGO in the land of Israel there lived a man named Jonah. He had a farm with a house, a field, and a garden. He had a small donkey to pull his plow.

One day after work he sat down in his garden to rest.

While he rested, he went to sleep. A voice wakened him. It was a voice like wind and rain and thunder.

"Arise!" it said. "Arise and go to Nineveh, that great city. Go and preach to the people against their wickedness!"

Jonah fell forward into the dust. He was trembling with fear, for he knew he had heard the voice of the Lord.

He lay in the dust. The voice did not speak again. He lifted his head.

He said to himself, "The Lord has spoken, and I must obey."

The Lord had said, "Arise!"

Jonah got to his feet.

But the Lord had said, "Arise and go to Nineveh."

Jonah asked himself, "Why must I go there?"

Nineveh was far away in the land of Assyria. The people of Assyria were enemies of Israel. It was true that they were wicked, but what was their wickedness to him?

He thought on these things, and his heart grew stubborn. He said in his heart, "Why should I preach to my enemies? I will not go."

Yet he knew the Lord would come again. The Lord would say, "You have not obeyed me. My punishment shall fall upon your head."

Jonah went into his house. He closed the door. "I will not go to Nineveh!" he said. "Neither will I stay to be punished by the Lord!"

He waited until night came. He went outside. He climbed upon his donkey and rode away.

All night he rode. As the sun came up, he fell in with a band of traders riding camels.

The traders were friendly. Jonah rode with them by day. He camped with them by night. They rode together until they came to Joppa, a city by the sea.

Jonah was far from home. Still he feared that even here the Lord might find him.

A ship was ready to sail from the harbor.

Jonah said to the captain, "Take me with you."

"Do you have money?" asked the captain.

Jonah went to the marketplace. There he sold his donkey for a handful of silver. He took the money back to the ship. He paid his fare and went on board.

The ship sailed. The sky was clear. The sailors were happy, and they sang.

But as the ship sailed beyond the harbor, the sky grew dark. A storm swept the sea.

The ship carried a cargo of grain. The sailors threw the cargo overboard to lighten the ship so that it would not sink.

The sailors believed in many different gods. Each man prayed to his god, "Save us—save us!"

Jonah was weary from his journey to Joppa. He had gone down into the ship and was fast asleep.

The captain went to him. He shook Jonah and said, "Arise, you sleeper. Pray to your God to save us."

On deck the sailors shouted to be heard above the wind.

"Someone on this ship has brought the storm upon us," said one.

"Let us cast lots," said another. "This will tell us who has brought the storm."

A sailor came with the lots. Each lot was a small square of wood with a number on it. He put them into a cup.

Two sailors stretched a cloth tightly between them. Each man in turn shook the cup so that only one lot fell out onto the cloth. Everyone watched to see who would shake out the lot with the low number.

The last of the sailors shook a lot from the cup.

"The low number has not fallen," said the men. "None of us has brought the storm."

Jonah and the captain came on deck.

"Will you cast with us?" asked the sailors.

The captain shook out one of the lots.

The men read the number on the lot. "It is not our captain who has brought the storm," they said.

A sailor held out the cup to Jonah.

Jonah drew back.

"You must cast with us," said the sailor.

Jonah took the cup. He shook it until one of the lots fell.

The men read the number on the lot. It was the low number.

"He has brought the storm!" they said. "It is Jonah—it is Jonah!"

They looked into his face. "Who are your people?" they asked. "What is your country?"

"I am a Hebrew from the land of Israel," he answered, "and I fear the Lord, the God of heaven."

Now he knew that even here the Lord had found him. He knew that nowhere on land or sea could he hide from the Lord.

The sailors asked him, "What shall we do to be saved?"

"Take me up and throw me into the sea," said Jonah. "Then the waters shall be calm, for the storm was sent because of me."

But no one wished to lay hands on Jonah.

The sky grew darker. The waves rose above the sides of the ship.

The sailors prayed to the Lord, "Let us not all be lost because of one man!"

Their voices could not be heard above the roar of the storm.

They waited no longer. They laid hands on Jonah and threw him into the sea.

At once the sky began to clear. The wind became a breeze, and the ship sailed in calm waters.

The sailors thanked God, even while they thought of Jonah. "He is lost," they said, "that we might be saved."

But Jonah was not lost. The Lord had caused a great fish to rise near the ship. As the waves closed over Jonah, the fish had swallowed him.

Jonah was alive inside the fish. He lived in terrible darkness, and he cried out to the Lord.

Three days and three nights passed. Then the Lord spoke to the fish. The fish opened its great mouth and cast Jonah out upon dry land.

Jonah felt the earth beneath him. He saw the sky and the sun, and he breathed the clean air. He gave thanks to the Lord.

Again the voice of the Lord spoke to him. "Arise," it said, "and go to Nineveh!"

This time Jonah obeyed.

He came to the gates of the city.

"Let me pass," he said, and the soldiers and guards made way for him.

Within the city he preached the words the Lord had given him: "After forty days Nineveh shall be destroyed!"

The people listened and were afraid.

The king himself came down from his throne. He dressed in rough sackcloth and sat in ashes. This was a sign that he had put aside his wicked ways. It was a sign that he believed in the word of God.

The other people of Nineveh dressed in sackcloth and rubbed themselves with ashes. They prayed to the Lord.

The Lord heard their prayers, and He forgave them. After forty days the city was not destroyed.

The people were joyful. They feasted together. They danced in the streets.

But Jonah was not joyful.

He had obeyed the Lord. He had preached to the people of Nineveh. Still he said to himself, "They are my enemies." He had not wished them to be saved, and he was angry because the Lord had not destroyed their city.

He went away into the desert nearby.

There he sat, in a poor shelter he had made of sticks. He looked toward Nineveh. He hoped that the Lord might yet destroy the city.

The Lord watched over Jonah. He sent a plant to grow beside the shelter.

In a single day the plant grew tall. It put forth branches and leaves. Its shade kept the burning sun from Jonah, and he was pleased.

That night he lay in the shadow of the plant. He saw the moon through its branches. He heard the whispering sound of the leaves. He began to love the plant as he would have loved a friend.

In the morning he looked into the branches, and he cried out. The leaves were dying.

"I must find water," he said.

But he quickly saw that water could not save the plant. Already the leaves had turned brown. The branches had drooped.

"Must you die? Must you die so soon?" said Jonah, and he wept.

The plant fell in a small, dry heap. An ugly worm crawled out of the stalk.

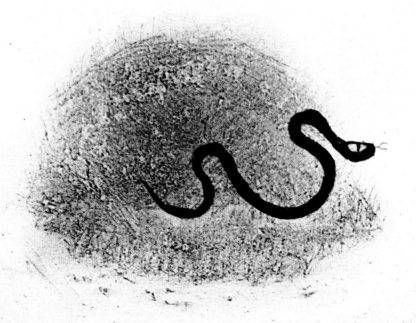

Jonah took up a stick. He tried to strike the worm, but it disappeared into the ground.

"Lord," he said, "You sent the worm to kill my plant. It was You, O Lord!"

Once more the sun beat down on Jonah's head. A burning wind began to blow.

He could not bear the heat of the wind and sun, and he said, "It is better for me to die than to live!"

The Lord spoke. "Is it well for you to be angry because of the plant?"

"Yes," said Jonah. "It is well for me to be angry."

The Lord said, "You have felt pity for something that grew and died in a day and a night. Is not the city far greater than the plant? Shall I not feel pity for Nineveh with its many thousands of people?"

Then Jonah was ashamed of his anger. He understood that the Lord loved all people, whether they be of Israel or Assyria or any other land. He bowed his head and thanked the Lord for His mercy.

About the Author

CLYDE ROBERT BULLA was born near King City, Missouri. He received his early education in a one-room schoolhouse, where he began writing stories and songs. After several years as a writer of magazine stories, he finished his first book, then went to work on a newspaper.

He continued to write, and his books for children became so successful that he was able to satisfy his desire to travel through the United States, Mexico, Hawaii, and Europe. He now lives in Los Angeles.

In 1962 Mr. Bulla received the first award of the Southern California Council on Children's Literature for distinguished contributions to that field. He has written more than thirty stories for young readers.

About the Illustrator

HELGA AICHINGER is one of the most successful of the youngest generation of European artists. Born in Linz, Austria, she began her career as a student of calligraphy and other graphic arts at the local Academy of Art. Her works have been purchased by the Museum of Modern Art in New York City, the Stedlijk Museum in Amsterdam, and many other museums and private collectors in Europe and America.

Her interest in children is revealed in the personal quality of her art. She addresses herself directly to the child, and opens a world to him in his own proportions.

Mrs. Aichinger lives with her husband at the edge of a forest in Austria.